RILA MONASTERY

This book has been commissioned by the RILA MONASTERY Ltd.

Margarita Koeva

RILA MONASTERY

BORINA

© Margarita Koeva, author, 1995
© Dimiter Angelov, photographer
© Vyara Kandjeva, photographer
© Antoniy Handjiysky, photographer
© Translation: Roumiana Delcheva
© BORINA Publishing House, Sofia

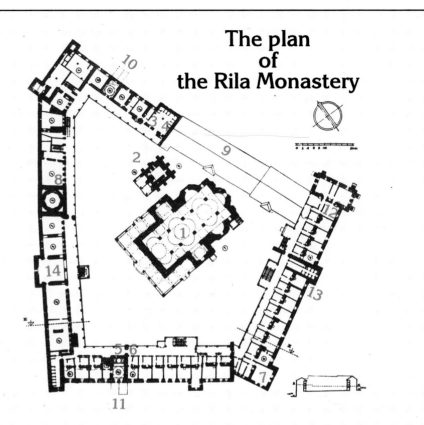

The plan of the Rila Monastery

1. The Church of the Nativity of the Virgin, the main church of the monastery.

2. Medieval tower with the Chapel of Transfiguration on the top level.

3. The Chapel of St John the Theologian on level three.

4. The Chapel of SS Sava and Simeon of Serbia on level four.

5. The Chapel of St John the Baptist on level three.

6. The Chapel of the Synaxis of Archangels.

7. The abbot's apartments: chambers, reception parlor with a chapel and the library of the monastery abbot.

8. The monastery kitchen: cellars and cooking rooms on the ground floor. Today it is a museum exposition of monastery life.

9. New guest house, a wing whose ground floor and basement house the monastery's museum of history.

10. The Samokov gate.

11. The Doupnitsa gate.

12. Replica (scale 100) of the cell in the Zographou Monastery in Mount Athos where Paisi of Hilendar wrote The Slav-Bulgarian History in 1762.

13. The old monastery refectory on the ground floor. Today it houses the Rila Monastery icon collection.

14. Guest rooms of the monastery, part of the ethnographic museum: the towns of Chirpan, Koprivshtitsa, Samokov, Gabrovo, Teteven on the northern wing top storey and the storey under it.

5

THE HEART OF RILA

The historic development of each nation involves the creation of cultural and material values. Some of them are the ultimate achievement of the mind or of the arts and enrich national as well as world culture. These are historic documents which are evidence of the creative endeavor of a nation and confirm unequivocally its right to historic existence and define its place in the development of world civilization. For the Bulgarians the Rila Monastery is one of the most outstanding proofs of the value of spiritual and artistic culture, the world of their predecessors. In the course of ten centuries it has been a literary and religious center which supported the internal stability of the nation in spite of the trials which interspersed its history. It was the second largest in the Balkans but in contrast to the monasteries on Mount Athos in Greece it always kept its doors wide open to everyone and performed socially useful work. The democratic nature of its activities was laid down in the Testament of its patron John of Rila (Ivan Rilski) who devoted his life of a hermit to a struggle for purity of the faith and for equality among people.

The monastery is located about 120 kilometers southwest of the Bulgarian capital Sofia, in the heart of the Rila Mountains from which it takes its name. A detour of the Sofia-Thessaloniki-Athens international motorway leads to the monastery which stands between the rivers Rilska and

The Rila Monastery - general view

7

Droushlyavitsa that act as its natural guards. It is surrounded by high mountain peaks, covered with centuries-old forests. Every visit to the monastery is a kind of a trip back in history while for the Bulgarians it is also homage to their history. Over the ten centuries since its foundation the Rila Monastery has emerged as a nationally revered holy place. With religious veneration the monastery monks have been writing, collecting and protecting manuscripts and old printed books, historic documents, royal gift charters, icons and church plate, gold-embroidered garments and gifts brought there by believers. The entire Orthodox world has recognized the monastery as a major religious center. That is evidenced by the numerous documents kept at the monastery library and the museum collections. Founded as a stauropegion monastery directly subject to the Patriarch it successfully preserved its independence through all the ups and downs of the Bulgarian Church and state. Church services have always been conducted in Bulgarian.

Over the centuries the Rila Monastery attracted many pilgrims. Even in the late 20th century hustle and bustle the monastery continues to be attractive for all who want to find peace for their soul and rest for their body. Every year about a million of pilgrims, tourists, scholars and men of art from different parts of the world visit the Rila Monastery to enjoy its beauty and get familiar with the fine art and religious collections. For these reasons in 1980 the International Federation of Travel Writers and Journalists (FIJET) distinguished it with the Golden Apple, the highest award for familiarization and cultural tourism. In 1983 the Rila Monastery was recorded on the List of World Cultural Heritage as a world cultural value. Again at that time it got the status of a national museum, so the government started subsidizing the museum collections, conservation and restoration of the wall paintings and the architectural heritage. A decree of the Council of Ministers of the Republic of Bulgaria reinstated the monastic status of the Rila Monastery in 1991, so today it is again the largest religious center in the Bulgarian lands.

Several generations of builders, craftsmen and artists have invested their work in the construction of the monastery buildings, putting up and decorating them with frescoes, wood carvings and stone ornaments. The result has been a monument of the artistic skill of the Bulgarian people. Built and maintained with the money and work donated by the entire Bulgarian population the Rila Monastery is a material expression of the hopes of the people put in devoted prayers. It radiates spiritual tranquillity and serene vitality.

10

THE SAINT OF RILA

St John of Rila, an icon,
17th century

St John of Rila. A fresco
in the Rila Monastery
main church gallery,
19th century.

The monastic community was founded by the medieval hermit Ivan who was later called Ivan Rilski. He chose seclusion which, he believed, would lead him to edification and service of God. Born in the seventies of the 10th century he witnessed the escalating moral decline of the rulers and notables of the First Bulgarian Kingdom during the reign of Tsar Peter (927-969). John of Rila took orders in a monastery in Mount Rouen, bade adieu to the relatively comfortable monastic life and retired to the Rila Mountains which was inaccessible in those days in order to translate into practice his ideas that Christianity should regain its genuine nature. As a champion of the purity of the Christian faith and of high moral standards the hermit of Rila advocated equality between people, renunciation of wealth that has been acquired in unfair ways; he pleaded for the underprivileged who are 'the salt of the earth' (Matthew, 5:13) for their labor and resignation and encouraged them. He renounced the earthly goods and 'multiplied the flock of Christ'* which he guided to the light of spiritual life. By and by his reform-minded ideas came to appeal to many and the cave in which he dwelt became a place of veneration for people from all Bulgarian lands.

His impact on his contemporaries was so big that Tsar Peter himself, the story goes, went to the Rila Mountains to pay homage to him and ask him for help, however, the saint

---

* Quotation from the Sredets Office to St John of Rila

refused to accept the wealthy gifts and to meet him.

His life as a hermit has been described in numerous works belonging to all genres of hagiographic fiction: long, short, extensive and panegyric lives and narratives about the translation of the saint's relics. It is presumed that the first life was written back in the 10th century, shortly after the death of St John of Rila when he was canonized. In Old Bulgarian literature there is an extensive cycle of songs and poems dedicated to the Rila saint. It includes more than 150 single-stanza songs and

The Assumption of the saintly father John of Rila. A fresco in the Chapel of St John of Rila, the Thaumaturgist, in the southern part of the main monastery church, 1847

11 canons organized into three large compositions commonly known as the offices. The first songs of this cycle were most likely written at the Rila Monastery soon after the death of its founder. We get information about his life and his worship from the seven extant lives, five of which are Slav and two are Greek, and from the offices in his honor. Here is a description of his lot contained in the long life from the Norus prologue, a brief text, written in Greek and translated in the Slav language in late 12th or early 13th century.*

'And this saint Ivan was during the days of the pious Tsar Peter and came from the village called Skiront.** He left his native place and came to a river called Rila. And there he found under the mountain a cave called Vurtopen and lived there long years. And the furies gave him much headache. And the apparitions - one was working people up against him, the other was shrieking under the stone.

The Return of the Relics of St John of Rila to the Monastery. A fresco in the narthex of the Church of SS Peter and Paul in the Orlitsa metochion of the Rila Monastery, 1863, painter Nikola I. Obrazopissov

---

* The text is in manuscript No 973 in the collection of Count A.S. Uvarov, GIM, Moscow
** Village of Skrino on the Strouma, where the remains of a church are found near the cave which according to the legend was the hermit's first abode

St John of Rila, the Thaumaturgist, with scenes from his life and depiction of the Rila Monastery with the Church of the Nativity of the Virgin. With implicative depiction of the churches around the monastery: the Presentation of the Virgin with the monastery graveyard, St Luke the Evangelist, the Assumption of the Virgin and the Assumption of St John of Rila (the church at the grave). Print, 1847

And he, bearing by the grace of God, yielded up his soul thanking God.

'When the pious Tsar Peter heard of his death he came and took his relics to place them in the town of Sredets. And he built a church there which he named after him and laid his relics here with great honors.

'And after 300 years the pious Tsar Assen set out and arrived in Sredets, took the saint's relics, translated them to Zagorie and laid them in the town of Trapezitsa, and built a church which he named after the saint. And the relics here give healing to this day.'

Some of the lives tell other stories but invariably note that St John of Rila invariably turned down the honors paid to him and readily gave help only to the poor and the truly unfortunate. His exploits as a hermit attracted a group of monks who settled near his cave. Around the year 931, at his instructions they laid down the foundations of the monastic community.

Shortly before his death the hermit of Rila wrote his Testament in which he expressed the ideas to which he had dedicated his life and instructed his followers.* Later his Testament became the basis of the monastery typicon, the regulations of the monastic community life, which is still in force.

The religious feat of the hermit of Rila was performed with „great unheard of bravery"**, with the awareness that it will be an

---

* The Testament of St John of Rila can be read in an extant early 19th century transcription as in the time of Turkish domination the monks hid the original to save in from destruction when the monastery was plundered. The original has not been found.

**Long Life of Ivan Rilski from the Sofia Prologue. Manuscripts in Bulgarian, Serbian, Moldavian, Wallachian and Russian.

example for the coming generations of clergy-
men and this makes him one of the eminent
names in the Middle Ages. His service of God
was also an effort to save national identity.
With courage and valor he devoted his life to
the cultural advancement of the Bulgarians.

The death of St John of Rila on August
18, 946 marked the beginning of his legend-
ary fame as a protector and the incarnation of
the hope of the Bulgarian people during the
centuries to come which were full of dramatic
trials and great misfortunes. Little wonder that
the authors of the lives and the hymns about

*St John of Rila and St
Gabriel of Lesnovo, a
hermit monk who lived
in the 11th century, a
follower of the Rila
saint. A fresco in the
Church of St John the
Divine in the eastern
wing of the monastery,
1821*

St John of Rila with scenes from his life: a detail from an icon, 17-18th century. King Peter and the messenger

him, anonymous writers or illustrious men of letters as was the Bulgarian Patriarch Euthymius, aimed to inspire confidence and fortitude in readers through the spiritual achievements of the saint and alleviate the burden that was the Bulgarian people's lot.

The prayer from the saint's long life is a vivid example of the Bulgarians' confidence that the saint of Rila, their protector and patron, would intercede:

Preserve the pure faith in us! (Bless our cities!) Pacify the world! (From hunger and perdition save us!) From fierce aliens guard

St John of Rila with scenes from his life, 17th-18th century

17

St John of Rila. An icon, 14th century, tempera. Rila Monastery Museum

us! (Console the old!) Guide the young! (Teach the insane sense!) Pity the widows! (Protect the orphans!) Nurture the children!

The glorious lifework of the hermit of Rila was recognized when he was canonized by the Eastern Orthodox Church and when his relics received homage, all of which medieval rulers availed themselves of to give legitimacy to their rule and power. Some time after his death the Bulgarian Tsar Peter I had the relics translated to a church that had been specially built in Sredets. The relics remained there till late 12th century. In 1183 the Magyar King Bela III had St John of Rila's relics translated to Ezstergom (Gran) in Hungary; however, before long the Bulgarians returned the relics. In late 12th century the Assenid dynasty who liberated the Bulgarian state from Byzantine occupation (1018-1185) organized solemn processions which translated the Bulgarian saint's relics to Turnovgrad which was the new royal city of the Second Bulgarian Kingdom. The translation gave legitimacy to their claims to the throne and to their right to be successors of the First Bulgarian Kingdom which ceased to exist when Byzantine rule was established in the Bulgarian lands. When in the latter half of the 14th century the Ottoman threat became tangible in the Balkan Peninsula, Euthymius, the Patriarch of Bulgaria, wrote a new excellent life of the Rila saint. He was regarded as an intercessor of the Bulgarians to God to whom they prayed during the cruel times of the Turkish invasion and the ensuing five-century long bondage (1393/96-1878).

In the hostile world of Moslem domination in which the Bulgarians were treated as 'rayah', ie population stripped of their national and religious identity, the worship of St John

of Rila became extremely common and Christians from all Balkan countries found refuge in the monastery that he had founded. In the first half of the 15th century even the monastic community made every effort and were extremely diplomatic when they tried to obtain permission to return the relics of the patron saint from the devastated ex royal city to the monastery. In 1469 an embassy of monks made a procession in the Bulgarian lands translating the relics. The translation of the relics attracted multitudes of Bulgarians, kindled hopes in the oppressed people,

St John of Rila. An icon from the Chapel of St Nicholas of the Rila Monastery main church, 1775

strengthened their confidence and reminded them of their Bulgarian identity. It was described by Dimitri Cantacuzenus and the writer Vladislav Grammaticus whose 'Short Novel about the Translation of the Relics of St John of Rila from Turnovo to the Rila Monastery' provides information about the plight of the Bulgarians under Turkish rule. This is the first historical work realistically describing the lot of the Bulgarian people at that time. Again St John of Rila performed a miracle as he instilled self-confidence and self-reliance in a multitude who evolved into a nation. Ever

A sheet of a prologue life of St John of Rila in the so called Dragan's Menaion, a 13th century manuscript in the library of the Bulgarian Zographou Monastery in Mount Athos

since the 15th century the relics have been in the monastery and believers pray the saint to intercede for them with God in times of trouble.

The Testament of the saint of Rila to his first followers was, is and will be a behest to all people in the world:

'As the grace of the Holy Spirit has brought us here together, so you try to live in the future in unanimity and concord, breathing together and enjoying together the eternal creation which God hath made for them that love Him. Woe to him that is alone when he falleth; for he hath not another to help him up...!'

St John of Rila with scenes from his life and depiction of the monastery and the return of the saint's relics to the monastery. An icon, latter half of the 19th century. Produced in Russia

THE RILA MONASTERY: A MONUMENT OF THE BULGARIAN PEOPLE'S BUILDING AND ARTISTIC SKILL

The Rila Monastery: part of the northern wing, the medieval tower and the central monastery church

The Rila Monastery: the courtyard

Ever since the Bulgarian Middle Ages the lands of the Balkan Peninsula have been the crossroads of many pilgrim routes leading to many holy places of the Christian world - Holy Land and the religious centers in the Balkans which were specially honored. In the course of centuries these routes formed an entangled network linking the towns with the monasteries. Around them appeared Chapels, sketae and metochia* where worshippers could find shelter, get food and protection. The Rila Monastery was a generally recognized holy place and as such was a center where several of the main pilgrim routes converged. There was one that came from Wallachia via Vidin, Sofia and Doupnitsa, to the Rila Monastery and Mount Athos; another from Kazanluk, Karlovo and Pazardjik via Samokov to the monastery and the Aegean area; and there was a third route from the western Bulgarian lands for pilgrims coming from Central Europe, Dalmatia and Serbia.

During the Bulgarian National Revival in the 18th century and especially in mid-19th

---

* *Chapel – a small house of prayer or church*
  Skete – a community of monks whose dwellings were built in the vicinity of a head church which was called 'kyria-kon' in the Byzantine style. The brethren of a skete obeyed the abbot of the monastery that the skete was attached to.
  Metochion –'associate', a small monastery or house for monks in a bigger monastery. During the Bulgarian National Revival (18th-19th century) the Rila Monastery metochia ran schools providing different levels of education.

25

century the number of pilgrims increased significantly and a large group of service buildings appeared around the monastery. The reception buildings of the metochia and the sketae along the river Rilska where there were places associated with the patron saint's worship were renovated during the same period. In this way there appeared several architectural ensembles whose purpose was to provide shelter and also to mentally prepare worshippers for their encounter with the holiest place in Bulgaria.

The first thing that visitors to the monastery see as they set foot on the Rila Mountains is the Orlitsa metochion which in the course of almost five centuries has been receiving pilgrims coming from the western parts of Bulgaria. In 1469 the Church of SS Peter and Paul was built to lay the relics of St John of Rila after they were returned to the monastery. In 1491 a group of icon painters decorated the church which had been redesigned in 1478. The building is still in place. The frescoes are extremely valuable since very few 15th century Bulgarian frescoes have survived. They are noted for their exquisite proportions, elongated figures, linear technique and aristocratic atmosphere characteristic of the medieval paintings in Hrelyo's Tower. Almost four centuries later, in 1863, Nikola Obrazopissets, a prominent National Revival painter, decorated the facade wall of the same church with a figural composition featuring The Translation of the Relics of St John of Rila. His intention was to recall why the church had been built. Precision and detail in clothes depiction are amazing; with the unaffected naivete, characteristic of the time, the artist portrayed the figures in the procession in contemporary dress. The landscape which evi-

St Luke the Evangelist. A fresco in the Chapel of the Synaxis of Archangels, western wing of the monastery, 1835. Painter Dimiter Molerov from Bansko

dently is very similar to that surrounding the metochion is as authentic as the dress.

Further upstream the road leads to a point which is the monastery's boundary and is guarded by a special building called the Watch Tower where the armed sentinels of the Rila Monastery were stationed. Those were specially drilled monastery servants and battle-steeled soldiers hired by the monastic community.

The next metochion which is closer to the monastery is called Pchelino. It was here that the Church of the Dormition of the Virgin

A diptych from the Rila Monastery, 17th century. In the left half: a Deesis - the Virgin, Jesus Christ and St John the Baptist; in the right half: two saints. National Museum of History, Sofia

was put up in late 18th century and decorated with frescoes in 1835 by Dimiter Molerov. This church keeps several of the earliest National Revival Period icons made especially for the monastery by Monk Zaharii from Mount Athos, and one of the valuable icons featuring the Rila hermit.

Two other groups of buildings rise high up in the mountain, northeast of the monastery. The buildings that are farther are on the site where the saint was buried. The buildings that are nearer are on the site where his nephew Luke is said to have been bitten by

A medallion from the wall painting frieze in the Chapel of the Synaxis of Archangels, western wing of the monastery. Painter Dimiter Molerov, 1835
The Church of the Assumption of St John of Rila that was built in mid-18th century and rebuilt in 1820. The eastern facade

a snake because his father did not allow him to become a disciple of the saint and a monk.

The Hermitage of St John of Rila is an original fusion of landscape and architecture. The cave where the hermit lived is in the rocks surrounded by a centuries-old forest. Dozens of visitors go there every day. The Church of the Repose of St John of Rila in whose narthex the tomb is supposed to have been is nearby. The old church on the site was rebuilt in 1820 and its walls were painted by Dimiter Molerov from Bansko and his son Simeon in

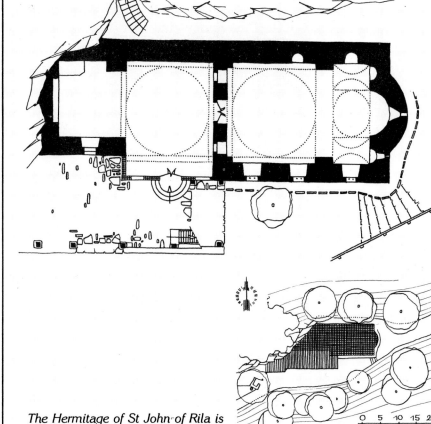

Plan: Ts. Stoichev

The Hermitage of St John of Rila is northeast of the monastery and farthest. It stands where the cave in which the hermit lived is and where he was initially buried. For this reason the Church of the Assumption of St John of Rila that was built in the 18th century is also known by the name The Church at the Grave. It was built ca 1746. It is a single nave, single apse building with a narthex. In 1820 it was rebuilt to become what it is today.

It was believed that a pilgrim who worms through the narrow crevice in the rock over the saint's cave will be purged of his or her sins. Sinners who can't will remain in the stone chimney without an indulgence. It is still believed and even today thousands of visitors who seek pardon for their sins creep up the steep stone steps that the feet of the saint of Rila touched.

Christ cures two possessed with devils. The Gospel According to St Matthew (8:28, 29, 30, 31, 32, 33). A fresco from the Church of St Luke the Evangelist in the Rila Monastery's Skete of St Luke, 1799

A fragment from the Last Judgment on the eastern wall of the narthex of the Church of St Luke the Evangelist in the Rila Monastery skete named after St Luke, 1798-1799

1844. The frescoes feature all the major events in the life of the hermit.

A path leads from the Hermitage to the monastery. Along the path there are several picturesque buildings built down a steep slope. This is the Skete of St Luke, also known as the New Hermitage. The oldest building here is the late 17th century Church of St Luke the Evangelist. It was painted in 1798-1799 when carvers from Bansko carved the iconostasis of wood. The surviving frescoes are a product of the brush of Toma Vishanov, called Molera* from Bansko who had studied in Central Europe and introduced baroque elements in Bulgarian ecclesiastical art, thus creating expressive and ethereal paintings which were new for the times. His personages with rosy cheeks and plump hands are radiant and vigorous in their moving admiration for the miracles of the God's world.

The second church of the ensemble,

---

* 'Moler' from German 'Mahler', as he had worked as an artist in a German-speaking country. Toma Vishanov was the progenitor of the Molerov family which produced several of the most illustrious names in 19th century church painting.

The iconostasis in the Church of St Luke the Evangelist in the Rila Monastery's Skete of St Luke, 1799. National Museum of History, Sofia

A detail from the iconostasis of the Church of St Luke the Evangelist

the Shroud of the Virgin, was put up in 1805 over the holy fountain by the builders Mihail and Radoitsa from the village of Rila. It has a large vestibule part of which is an outdoor structure whose walls were painted by Toma Vishanov in 1811. They feature a cycle on the subject of the Ordeals of the Soul. Vishanov introduced the spirit of the time and the new forms which he had discovered in the traditional form. Another National Revival Period painter, Hristo Dimitrov from Samokov, introduced scenes from everyday life and didactic scenes such as 'Righteous and Un-

A cross of the iconostasis of the Church of St Luke the Evangelist featuring Christ Crucified and the symbols of the New and Old Testament, the four gospel writers in the four ends of the cross and death which has been defeated by the Cross sacrifice at the feet of Jesus

The Church of
St Luke the Evangelist

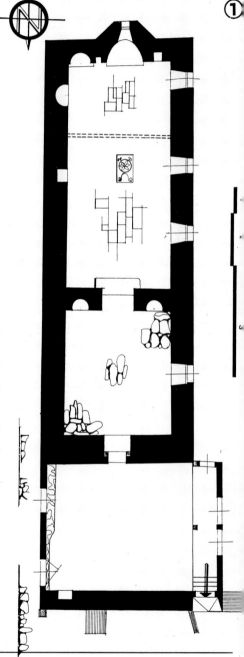

Храма „СВ. ЕВангелист Лука" е
най-старата сграда В едноименния
скит на Рилския манастир. Той се на-
мира на около два километра източ-
но от манастира като през него ми-
нава планинската пътека, Водеща
към постницата на Рилския светец.
Според легендата тук е починал,
ухапан от змия, племенникът на СВ.
ИВан Рилски – Лука, който, подлъган
от зли сили, изоставил монашеския
живот. На това място бил изграден
параклис, а по-късно и църква, посве-
тена на неговия светец покровител.
Наличието на средновековни зидове
В двора на скита и В основите на
днес съществуващите църкви пот-
Върждава наличието на историчес-
ка истина В старинната легенда.

Строителната история на църкВата „СВ. ЕВангелист Лука" крие из-
Вестни загадки. Поради стръмния
терен сградата, която от север е
едноетажна, В южната си част има
два равностойно Високи етажа. В
долния от тях е запазен средновe-
ковен градеж, който оформя нещо
като масивно засводена зала. Към
нея са прибавени по-нови части пре-
дназначени да служат като основа
на църквата, изградена през XVIII В.
Същинската църква се развива на
горния етаж и се състои от масивно засводен наос, тристенна апси-
да и обширен, също масивно засводен притвор. От западната страна
на притвора е прибавено преддверие,
което свързва църквата с училище-
то, построено през 1864 г. Наосът,
олтара и притвора са изписани през
1798-99 г. В олтара стенописите

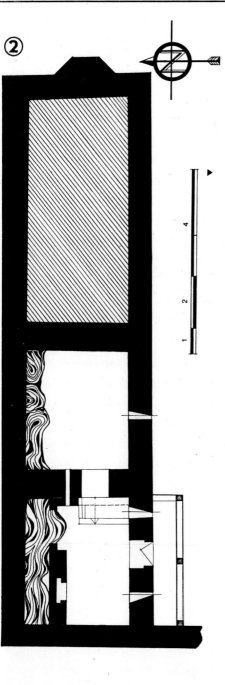

②

принадлежат на Тома Вишанов – Молера, а останалите са рисувани от зографи, очевидно добре познаващи художествените традиции на Атон. Те са с високи художествени качества, но нямат новаторския повей, отличаващ живописта на Тома Вишанов.

На север от църквата „Св. Евангелист Лука", върху висока площадка е построена църквата „Покров Богородичен". Тя е издигната през 1805 г. върху основи на по-стара сграда, включвайки свещения извор (аязмо), бликащ в основите ѝ. Църковната сграда е еднокорабна, едноапсидна, масивно засводена, с голямо, полуоткрито преддверие. Стенописи покриват стените и свода на наоса и стените на преддверието, към което дървен чардак се надвесва над аязмото. Живописта датира от 1811 г., зографите, между които е и Тома Вишанов принадлежат на Банската живописна школа.

Архитектурният ансамбъл завършва с училищната сграда, построена по идея на Неофит Рилски. Тя е най-късна по време. Долепена до църквата „Св. Евангелист Лука", сградата е също като нея двуетажна на юг. Тя се състои от голяма зала за лекции, до която е и жилището на учителя и складови помещения в приземието. В нея големият възрожденски просветител е преподавал на своите ученици според правилата на създадената от самия него система на светско, не само църковно, обучение.

righteous Confession' and 'Going to the Fortuneteller' (1799).

In 1864 Neophit Rilski, a distinguished National Revival educator, designed and added a school building to the Church of St Luke where he opened his own school which for a short time was famous all over Bulgaria. Although he was a clergyman and an abbot of the monastery, he was the first champion of secular education in his day. What he did for the cause of the Bulgarian National Revival can compare with what St John of Rila did in the Middle Ages.

Royal doors of the iconostasis of the Church of St Luke the Evangelist featuring the Annunciation in the upper tier and St John Chrysostom and St Basil the Great in the lower tier

A small group of buildings that are enclosed by a stone wall is very near to the monastery. It includes the cemetery church and the monastery ossuary, several buildings with living premises and the monastery cemetery. The cemetery church of the Presentation of the Virgin where the brethren served their funeral service dates probably from early 17th century. Like most medieval ossuaries is it on two levels and is a small lavishly decorated one-aisle church. Its frescoes from 1795 are characteristic of the style of a group of Bulgarian artists who worked on Mount Athos during the 18th and 19th century. Its iconostasis is noted for its elegant proportions and beautiful wood carving.

A sorceress. A fresco from the vestibule of the Church of St Luke the Evangelist in the Rila Monastery's Skete of St Luke, 1799

Offices and service rooms occupy the eastern sector of the monastery. Today, as in the past, they are quite numerous since the monastery has always had an infrastructure of its own. The monastery bakery built in the 19th century when the bakery in the monastery's main courtyard could no longer provide for the pilgrims is most interesting. It is a free-standing structure. Both its architecture and decoration are similar to the other facades of the monastery.

The long history of the buildings in the Rila Monastery goes back to late 10th century when the monastic community that the Rila hermit had founded put up the first buildings not far from the cave which he occupied. The story is that they were called Belite Kelii (The White Cells) but where exactly they stood is not clear. The remains of walls around the Old Hermitage and near the Skete of St Luke show that the monks moved their abode several times, getting closer and closer to the monastery's present site between the rivers Rilska and Droushlyavitsa. They probably

The Church of
the Presentation of the Virgin

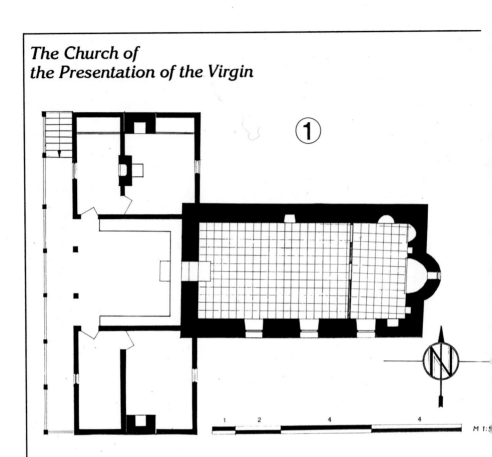

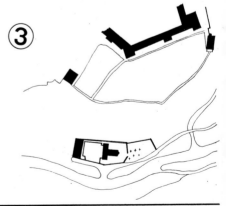

The Church of the Presentation of the Virgin is south of the monastery, in the proximity of the river. It is intended to be the ossuary of the monks and architecturally is a medieval two-level ossuary church. Three successive stages can be traced in the construction. The first stage, probably from Late Middle Ages, produced the two-level stone body of the church consisting of two single nave and single apse spaces with solid vaulting one above the other. The lower level is to hold the bones of the monks who died and the upper level is for service. A two-

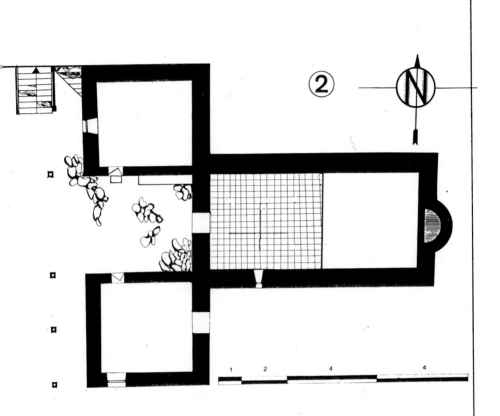

②

N

| 1 | 2 | | 4 | | 4 |

storey annexe with one room looking north and one room looking south on each storey was added to the stone church in the 1790s, leaving large half-open space in front of the western wall for the church. Thus big outer narthexes were formed in front of the ossuary and the church proper where memorial service of the dead is served. In 1795 the church was painted all over and an iconostasis of carved wood was put probably to replace an older one. In the latter half of the 19th century when accommodation, religious and farm buildings were built and the yard was surrounded by open balconies, a wooden gallery balcony was attached to the ossuary and thus the western part of the church was architecturally integrated in the graveyard ensemble.

Hrelyo's Tower

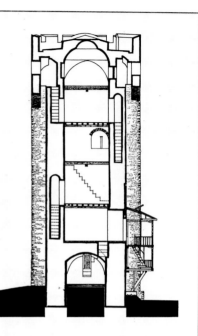

Medieval construction in the monastery is represented by the defense tower which is in a perfect state of preservation. The memorial inscription on the stone walls tells that the tower is dedicated to „the holy father John of Rila and the Virgin called Ossenovitsa." It was built in 1334-35 by the feudal lord Hrelyo Dragovol.

The 23-meter tall tower stands on an almost square base and like most structures of this type, is supplied with all the premises to endure long assault and siege. The five levels are for accommodation and defense and there is a dungeon in the basement. Originally a ladder was taken out and in in case of danger. The merlons on the roof and the embrasures over the gate and on the walls from where defenders could pour out burning liquids or hurl heavy stones at the enemy made it virtually invincible.

The Chapel of the Transfiguration on the top level consists of two premises covered with blind domes. The smaller premise functioned as a naos. The dome features Christ Emmanuel and the walls, a symbolic iconographic picture of the Divine Wisdom. Three scenes from the life of St John of Rila have been added to the main subject and are the earliest part of the painted life of the Bulgarian saint.

The paintings in the narthex illustrate verses from Davidic psalms 148, 149 and 150.

In the time of bondage fire damaged the wall paintings which in 1792 were covered with a new coat of paint. Today visitors can see them again owing to the efforts of a team of Bulgarian restorers led by Prof. L. Prashkov.

chose this place because it could be better fortified. We have scanty information about the place before the 14th century. The lot of the monastic community can only be guesswork on the basis of Tsar Ivan Shishman's late 14th century gift charter which mentions that the monastery was getting donations from the Bulgarian Tsars Ivan Assen and Koloman who ruled during the 13th century.

In the 14th century Hrelyo Dragovol, a feudal lord whose domain comprised the lands around the river Strouma, transformed the monastery into a solidly fortified and im-

A gift charter of the Bulgarian king Ivan Shishman, 1378. Parchment measuring 170/28.5 centimeters. The golden seal fixed in the lower part of the charter is 4.2 centimeters in diameter

posing architectural ensemble. This is evidenced by the remains of solid walls in the southwestern corner of the monastery courtyard unearthed during archaeological excavations and also by the prominent tower which still stands in the courtyard and by the paintings in the monastery church built by the feudal lord and surviving until mid-19th century. Fragments of the frescoes and the exquisitely carved wooden door are now kept in the monastery museum. Although small it was richly decorated and was fit to keep the relics of St John of Rila. After Hrelyo Dragovol the Rila

The Rila Monastery: the medieval tower and the main monastery church

Monastery became the largest feudal domain in the Bulgarian lands and continued to be such during the centuries of Turkish domination.

At the end of the 14th century the Bulgarian Kingdom fell under Ottoman rule. That was the greatest misfortune ever to strike the Bulgarian people. It changed their fate, slowed down their development by centuries and forcibly broke off their contacts with Europe. That changed also the lot of the monastery. Although the Turkish sultans gave the monastery protection charters during different periods it was often subjected to attacks and plunder. In mid-15th century the monks were forced to leave it and it was only at the end of that century that three brothers from the village of Granitsa managed to restore the buildings and prepare them for the great event, the return of the relics of St John of Rila from Turnovo to the monastery that he had founded. Large-scale building works began some time during mid-18th century and after 1816 the monastery already had high solid residential buildings which enclosed the courtyard in the shape of an irregular quadrangle. The medieval tower and the main church are in the center of this quadrangle.

January 13, 1833 was one of the most tragic dates in the long history of the monastery. The fire which broke out during the night destroyed almost completely the residential quarters. That was a national calamity and soon people began to send donations for the monastery's restoration. Thousands of masons, carpenters and auxiliary workers arrived to work and did not get payment for their work. Only in a couple of years the buildings were restored. The spontaneous effort, determination and will of the

The oldest print featuring the monastery was produced in Vienna in 1791. It depicts, schematically though, the medieval Church of the Virgin of Ossenovo that was built in 1342-1343, in the time of the feudal lord Hrelyo Dragovol. This depiction and Neophit Rilski's description allow the hypothetical reconstruction of the first monastery church which was a three-conch domed church whose under-dome interior measured approximately 6.00/6.00 meters which are the dimensions of the late 18th century iconostasis that has survived. The iconostasis was placed in the medieval church when it was redesigned and rebuilt (1780-83). A second so called midnight area with a dome too was west of the naos for the mandatory night service of the monks. Two shallow chapels opening to the midnight area were added during reconstruction which has not been dated. The next extension was in late 18th century when the iconostasis which is today in the southern chapel of the main monastery church was made. Another premise with an open gallery surrounding it from three sides was added west at about the same time. Despite all the reconstruction the church was small for the needs of the monastery in the 19th century. In 1834 the monks decided to pull it down and replace it by a monumental church which is still in place.

The church was painted all over. The monastery museum keeps fragments of the medieval paintings. Stylistically they are akin to the paintings created in the first half of the 14th century probably by the painters who painted the Chapel of Transfiguration on the top level of the defense tower .

Some of the wall paintings were transferred to the monastery's newly built guest rooms and some, to wood shields. The portrait of St John of Rila in a niche on the eastern wall of the Koprivshtitsa room is of special interest.

thousands transformed architecture into a material expression of the most cherished desire of the Bulgarian people - beauty, freedom and consolidation.

Three Bulgarian master builders (purvomaistori*) were in charge of the construction works whose scale was unprecedented in those times. They were Alexi from the village of Rila, called Alexi Rilets who built the northern parts of the east and the west wings, Milenko from the village of Radomir who built the south wing and 'architecton' Pavel from the village of Krimin who built the church

The Rila Monastery: general view

which at the time was the largest in the Balkans. The decoration of the main church, the chapels and the visitors' rooms was completed by 1870. At that time the monastery was as we know it today. There have been some recent changes in this majestic ensemble. The part of the east wing which was left unfinished has been replaced by a new one whose ground floor is now the monas-

---

* *Purvomaistor was a title granted to the best qualified builders who had proved their skills. During the National Revival Period there were also other titles: ousta, and architecton, borrowed from Turkish and Greek.*

tery's museum and one of the ground premises of the south wing has been reconstructed to fit in a replica of the cell of Paisi of Hilendar, the ardent Bulgarian enlightener who in the fifties of the 18th century wrote The Slav-Bulgarian History, the manifesto of the Bulgarian National Revival.

The first encounter with the architecture of the Rila Monastery is deeply moving. The smooth stone walls are some 20 meters high and create the impression that it is like a fortress. At regular intervals they are supported by solid flying buttresses lending the walls

The facade of the monastery's southern wing

greater loftiness. The color of the external walls harmonizes with the cold tonality of the surrounding landscape of high snow-topped mountain peaks, dark green pine forests and stone-walled river beds. The only bright spots are the porticos in front of the two entrances - the Doupnitsa and Samokov gates named after these towns as the roads leading to the monastery passed via them.

This picturesque architecture of the courtyard is in glaring contrast with the external design. The encircling multistoried wings are girdled with arcades varying in height and

The Rila Monastery: the southern wing and the main Church of the Nativity of the Virgin

roped with the exception of the latest east wing, by a wooden gallery. The rhythm of the arcades is broken by numerous bay windows and thick curtain walls. Looking at just one single part of the facade one gets the illusion of incredible diversity and wealth. The play of light and shade and the broad open stairs add up to this purposefully achieved effect. Certain details may provoke the objections of more refined admirers but as a whole the monastery irresistibly fascinates visitors. The decorative paintings are an integral part of architecture. Every part of the inside walls, of the columns and the arches is covered with ornaments or frescoes. The polychrome decorations fill up the spacious courtyard with the warmth of the carmine, the softness of the ochre and the play of the numerous black and white spots. The magic effect is staggering. It reflects the artistic experience of the Bulgarians, and is an expression of their attitude to the secrets of the world and the mythology firmly embedded in their minds.

The medieval tower is integrated in the ensemble by way of balancing the different volumes and the use of elements of its decoration as the basis for the decorative paintings: the brick semicircles which support the overhanging upper story of the tower are repeated by painted red bricks on the arches encircling the monastery courtyard. The inscriptions with bricks on the monastery facades and the facade of the monastery bakery have been borrowed from Hrelyo's memorial inscription on the western wall of the tower.

The imposingly big structure of the tower whose monumentality is further enhanced by the austere shape is incorporated into the National Revival architecture and

A fresco in the western room of the Chapel of the Transfiguration of Christ in the monastery's medieval tower. The group of warriors. Davidic psalm 148, 14th century

Frescoes on the dome of the eastern premise of the Chapel of the Transfiguration of Christ in the medieval tower. The pictures treat the Old Testament topic „Sophia, the Divine Wisdom". Christ Emmanuel (14th century) is dominating decoration by a 19th century light building. It is oriented towards the main church which stands next to it but does not clash with the effect created by the tower which is an almost 23 meter high square. It has five levels, an underground hiding place and a chapel on the top level. It was built to protect the monastic community and the family of the feudal lord Hrelyo and is a characteristic medieval structure. There were such towers in all the larger Balkan East Orthodox monasteries from the 12th to the 14th century. Hrelyo's Tower differs from them in that it has some remarkable

wall paintings which are in the Chapel of the Transfiguration of Christ. Its wall paintings are among the few surviving 14th century Bulgarian masterpieces. Time has spared them and the fire has destroyed only the wooden parts. They have been well conserved and now we are able to admire the complex religious and symbolic world of the medieval Bulgarians. The depictions reveal what notions people had centuries ago of Divine Rationalism and Divine Wisdom (St Sophia). They are noted for the purity of line, exquisite colors and the surprisingly simple yet perfect compositional

The Rila Monastery: a medieval fortress built by the feudal lord Hrelyo Dragovol, 14th century

Frescoes in the Chapel of the Transfiguration of Christ. The pictures in the lower tier illustrate the theme from king David's psalms 148, 149 and 150 „Praise ye the Lord"; the intermediary tier contains 8 figural scenes and the dome is taken by Christ the Ruler of the Universe

approach. The elongated figures, with beautiful hands and supple gestures, are an inseparable part of the small chapel. They fill it up with the quaint music of the group of players on the western wall as they take the visitor on a trip through time and space to the very nature of existence.

Apart from the scenes which were an inseparable past of the accepted East Orthodox iconography there are three which relate events from the life of St John of Rila. They have been badly damaged by time but are nonetheless the earliest painted hagiographic

scenes* about the saint of Rila. They date back to 1335 and along with the first portrait of the saint in the Church of St Nicholas in the village of Boyana, are valuable documents about how much he was adored in medieval times.

The Church of the Nativity of the Virgin is the monastery's main church and the core of the architectural ensemble.** Its construction began in 1835. That was an event of paramount importance for the entire Bulgarian nation. The innovative daring and the flexibility with which tradition has been interpreted

A fresco from the western premise of the Chapel of the Transfiguration of Christ. A group of musicians and dancers. Psalm 150 (3,4,5)

in the architectural design of this imposing church reveals the nature of art during the National Revival Period.

This church building is unique in the Balkans. It was constructed by the then widely known master builder Pavel from the village of Krimin who had worked on Mount Athos and

---

* *Depiction of events from the life of the saint.*

** *Main monastery church (catholicon, Byzantine). The major church of each monastery in the center of the monastery courtyard. In monastic parlance catholicon also stands for the central part of the space of the same church.*

The main facade of the main monastery church, the Nativity of the Virgin

from where he borrowed the original spatial design of the church. The compositional scheme includes medieval elements and baroque spatial principles, an approach which distinguishes Bulgarian church architecture and whose features are observed in the art of the epoch. On the basis of the quincunx plan that was conventional in Byzantine architecture the Bulgarian architect put up a church whose plan comprises three cores that are braided rhythmically in a baroque manner par excellence. Overlapping produces undivided and prominent inner space which is made up of rhythmically connected space groups. That space grabs visitors on entering the church. The three large domes allow the light to center on the gilded screen of the iconostasis which separates the congregation and the sanctuary where only the initiated are let in. The royal doors in the center of the iconostasis is the only place through which at some point of liturgy the altar space can be seen by the congregation. The reliquary of the monastery, the wooden chest with the relics of St John of Rila, is by the royal doors. The rich decorations of the carved iconostasis, the

The main monastery church: interior. The small iconostasis in the foreground, left, with the miracle-working icon of the Virgin of Ossenovo with holy relics and the pulpit of the church. The central iconostasis in the distance

shimmer of the gilded parts, the brilliance of the icons on it and ingenuity of light fixing put the finishing touch to the whole interior decoration which is so diverse and so integral in diversity that conveys the national and religious message in an absolutely new way.

The central iconostasis is the work of a group of wood carvers who worked under the supervision of Atanas Teladour. They spent three years working on it, from 1839 to 1842, investing it with the experience of several generations of carvers who founded the Bulgarian school of wood carving. The size and composition of the iconostasis are unrivaled in the Balkans. Same as architecture it follows the traditions of the school combining time-honored elements with a modern plastic approach. The intent of the master was to have it as the crowning element of space and as a unifying element emphasizing the center of the basilica. The carving which covers it from end to end is somewhat different from the carving on other iconostases. Here everything is bigger to harmonize with the large space inside the church. The carving differs from filigree miniature and is more like sculpted rather than carved.

The colors of this huge iconostases are in harmony with the rich colors of the interior. In the dim church space framed by the painted walls, illuminated by the hundreds of candles burning in the candleholders, the iconostasis' gilded carved surfaces glitter and reflect upon the brightly colored icons merging with the church space forming a complete artistic whole.

There are two other iconostases which belong to the side chapels and thus stand aloof from the central space. One of them, the iconostasis of the Chapel of St John of Rila,

0 - 1 2 3 4 5 6 7 8 9 ·10 м

The Church of the Nativity of the Virgin

1. Altar of the main church. The most important part of the church, the „divine church" which only priests can enter. Dedicated to the Nativity of the Virgin.
   a) central part - bema
   б) prothesis
   B) diaconicon (the plate receptacle)
   в) Holy Throne

2. Iconostasis. In the Eastern Orthodox churches it is a screen separating the altar and the congregation. It symbolizes the „celestial facade" and is covered by several tiers of icons.
   a) royal doors
   б) deacon's doors

3. Choirs - added to the basic part of the naos for two groups of singers performing the Divine Service.

4. Naos. The middle part of the church for the congregation and the clergy who perform the chants and conduct the reading of communal prayers.

5. The Chapel of St Nicholas of Myra in Lycia. Northern chapel of the church with a separate altar and a possibility for its own approach to the gallery.

6. The chapel dedicated to St John of Rila the Thaumaturgist. The last iconostasis from the old Church of the Virgin of Ossenovo from late 18th century and the oldest icons in the church painted by Zahari the Monk like the icon of St John of Rila from 1791, are kept there.

7. A reliquary holding the relics of the saint of Rila.

8. The heart of King Boris III was buried here in 1993 in a special chamber.

9. Galleries or parvises or catachumena. Open space surrounded by a colonnade from the direction of the yard covered with plenty of blind domes (calottes) and lavishly decorated with wall paintings.

the Miracle Worker, is of special interest. There is strong indirect evidence that it is the iconostasis of the medieval church which used to be on that site. The iconostasis was made in the 18th century when the church was renovated again. The form of carving and the composition that are typical of several late 18th century icons prove that.

Four small single-icon stands complete the setting in the central area and together with the carved archbishops' thrones and the pulpit put the finishing touch.

The wall paintings in the naos and in the

The main monastery church of the Nativity of the Virgin: interior. Archive photo, 1904

cloister testify to the advancement of art during the second half of the 19th century. They feature 1200 scenes which are a real gallery of Bulgarian National Revival Period painting. They beam with serenity and buoyancy and stick only formally to the requirements of the canon. Numerous minute details in the garments, in the architectural setting or landscape where the figures are positioned, show that the painters have been copying real life. The personages are expressively sensual.

The numerous donors' portraits indicate that at that time the national self-confidence was changing and people were prepared to make sacrifices so as to honor the national relic and thereby immortalize themselves. They also testify to a major process characteristic of the Bulgarian National Revival art. The secular attitude to art was beginning to strike roots in the very heart of ecclesiastical art. The names, the social status and even the gestures of the portrayed individuals differ from those in older donors' portraits. Among them are the portraits of Dougan and Rada from Koprivshtitsa, chorbadji (master) Vulcho, a prominent donor to the Bulgarian Zographou monastery in Mount Athos, Maria and Mihail from Teteven. Although their figures still express the time-honored rigid devotion and piety which are realistically portrayed, their expression suggests self-esteem and joie de vivre.

As was the custom the scenes painted on the facade walls of the main monastery church treat subjects associated with afterlife and the last judgment. Those depicting the ordeals of sinners are most interesting. They taught moral lessons to the people during the National Revival. The virtuous are protected while the thieves, the drunkards, the dishonest

Portraits of the donors Vulko and Rada Chalukov from Koprivshtitsa in the Chapel of St John of Rila, the Thaumaturgist of the main monastery church of the Nativity of the Virgin

merchants and the lewd are grotesquely ridiculed. Satire is a powerful weapon and here it has been put to best use. The primary force of the portrayals comes from the combination of the primitive and the sublime. The result is vigorous and powerful art, instructing people how to live righteously here on earth.

The wall paintings in the Church of the Nativity of the Virgin were made by the most prominent Bulgarian painters at the time. Most of them were from Samokov where the artists of the Zograph (Painter) family, Zahari Zograph, Dimiter H. Zograph and Stanislav Dospevski, worked. In the 1840s they were joined by Ivan Obrazopissets and his son Nikola Obrazopissets. There was a group of artists from Bansko led by Dimiter Molerov, and many other unknown assistants. In the course of several years, at the cost of great effort, to quote Neophit Rilski, they completed the church interior walls, the domes, the facades hidden under the arcade and its

The main monastery church of the Nativity of the Virgin: the outer gallery

small domes and produced 40 large icons for the iconostases and many other smaller ones. In view of the common goal the artists of this large team did their best to formulate a com-

Frescoes from the outer gallery of the main monastery church of the Nativity of the Virgin, 1844

mon idea so it is rather difficult to define with certainty who did what. There is unity in the idiom of the wall paintings. They form a motley mosaic covering the walls and the domes, and are perceived not as an addition to the interior but rather as the main element of the general artistic concept. Here lies their greatest merit.

The premises with religious function that are associated with the main church include the four chapels in the monastery's residential wings. They were and are used for religious service for which the main church is too big. Those are medium-sized rooms with altars and some have a narthex.

The Chapel of St John the Theologian in the monastery's east wing is the earliest one and a survivor of the great fire. The reconstruction incorporated the chapel into the new building and today the chapel stands as it was originally built in 1816. The chapel was decorated with frescoes in 1821 by icon painters from Bansko and Samokov. The iconostasis exhibits the same features of team work. While the composition is noted for its baroque treatment, characteristic of the woodcarvers from Samokov, the woodcarvings covering the ar-

Donors' portraits of grandpapa Iani and granny Stefana from the village of Badino in the Chapel of St Nicholas of the main monastery church of the Nativity of the Virgin, 1841

Wall decoration of the central calotte over the main entrance of the Church of the Nativity of the Virgin

The archangel Michael torments the soul of a rich man. A fresco from the outer gallery of the Church of the Nativity of the Virgin, 1844

chitectural elements are reminiscent of the techniques employed by the masters from Bansko. Although the iconostasis is not very big it conveys a sense of grandeur which is created by the lavishly used colors, the gold-covered carvings, the lucid silver mounted icons and deep tones, of the frescoes covering all the walls and the vault. The chapel is a consummate work of art.

The Chapel of SS Sava and Simeon of Serbia built in 1834-1835 and painted much later by Dimiter Zograph and his son Zaphir who after graduating from the Academy of

ΑΠΛΗ

ГРИШЕДШЇИ ВЪ ШЕСТЫИ ЧАС

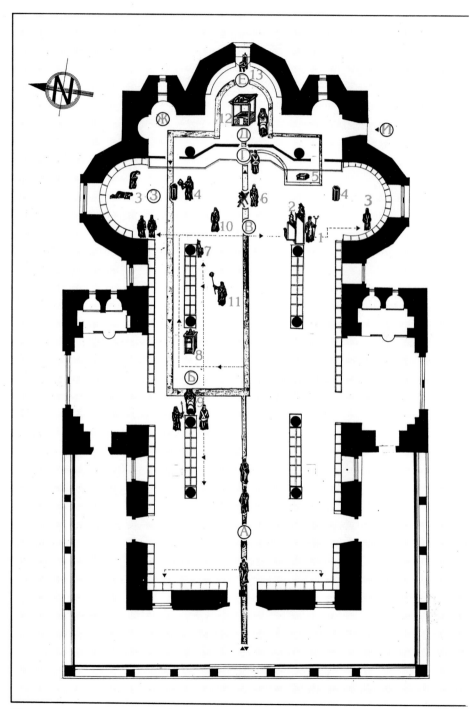

Eastern Orthodox liturgical practices were completed in the 14th century. The Rila Monastery comprises all elements established in the thousands years of monastic life. The plan shows the major service places in the main church of the monastery:

А - the place for genuflectory litany.

Б - the place where the miracle-working icon of the Virgin stands to which the monks bow when they enter the church and to which the priests and the candle server bow during the „small" and „great" presentation.

В - the place of blessing during Divine Service, the so-called Blessing at Presentation.

Г - the place of the deacon during Divine Service.

Д - the place of the priest during Divine Service, in front of the Holy Throne.

Е - the place of veneration of the Holy Place.

Ж - the place of preparation of the offerings of the proskomidia.

З - a northern choir where vespers are performed.

И - entrance into the altar for the priests and deacons.

1 - the place of the Rila Monastery abbot.

2 - the throne of the bishop or the abbot of the monastery.

3 - northern and southern choirs, parts of monastery churches where Divine Service is sung.

4 - a lectern - reading-desk in church where the service books are put and where a reader reads during Divine Service.

5 - the reliquary holding the relics of St John of Rila.

6 - a mobile lectern for Gospel reading in the center under the dome.

7 - a lectern by the first column in the naos (the core of the church) for the performance of the liturgy of the 9th hour.

8 - a small iconostasis with the miracle-working icon of the Virgin of Ossenovo.

9 - the priest, deacon and candle-bearer during the „small" and „great" presentation.

10 - canonarch, a singer who gives the lines and tune to the other singers. He faces the singers.

11 - the censer server, the monk who lights and extinguishes the censer.

12 - the Holy Throne.

13 - the High Place or Upper Place, the bishop's throne and the synthronon in the central altar apse

Depiction of the Virgin of Ossenovo, the medieval church of the monastery. A detail from an engraving engraved in Moscow, 1800

Fine Arts in St Petersburg was known as Stanislav Dospevski and was one of the first university-trained artists in Bulgaria, is one level up in the same wing. When in 1846 he was doing the frescoes in the chapel he was still very young and was under the strong influence of the traditions observed by his family. Here again the iconostasis is polychromatic and its icons markedly brilliant. As a result the whole chapel seems to be flooded with light and appears a lot larger than it really is. The effect is characteristic of baroque art. The Bulgarian master painters were able to achieve this effect thanks to their liberal attitude to convention and tradition. That was the underlying principle of Revival art.

The other two chapels of St John the Baptist and the Synaxis of the Archangels are in the west wing of the monastery. The larger of the two is on the fourth level and was built in 1834. It was painted a year later by Toma Vishanov's son Dimiter Molerov. Dimiter Molerov's wall paintings and all of his other works for that matter are monumental and of high artistic standard. However, the chapel is small and badly lit and the artistic effect can-

The Entry into Jerusalem. An icon, early 19th century. Samokov school, wood, tempera

not be compared to that of the chapels in the east wing.

The Chapel of St John the Baptist is one level below and has the same plan but lacks Dimiter Molerov's splendid paintings. The wall paintings and the iconostasis are characteristic examples of popular art but do not have the fascinating primitive verve which transforms them into singular works of art.

National Revival decorative arts most closely approximate the fascination of folk art. The various ornaments have been borrowed from medieval Bulgarian art but have been

Frescoes from the Chapel of St Sava and Simeon of Serbia in the eastern wing of the monastery, 1844-1846

treated quite freely. The artistic effect of this fusion reflects the outstanding vitality of Bulgarian art, its flexibility, resilience and ability to adapt. The same experienced artists did the monastery's decorations. For this reason decorations harmonize with architecture and figural painting.

The monastery keeps hundreds of examples of decorative arts - medallions, landscapes, ornamental friezes, painted architectural elements. The decorations on the monastery's two gates stand out.

The monastery was built as a fortress

Cherubim. A fresco from the Church of the Assumption of St John of Rila (the old hermitage), 1820

Hrelyo's Tower, a 14th century inscription

A fountain in the Rila Monastery courtyard. The basin is supported by two lion sculptures, 1816

and for this reason it has only two entrances that are guarded by solid iron-studded gates. When the gates were closed, the monastery became a real castle. However, that function has been discreetly veiled by means of architecture and painting to stress the monastery was a democratic institution which is open to all who come for prayer or cure. Hence the lavish decoration on the entrances which are like tunnels intersecting the width of the wings. Although the decoration is not exquisite it has the impact that the artists were after. On entering the colonnaded porticos that

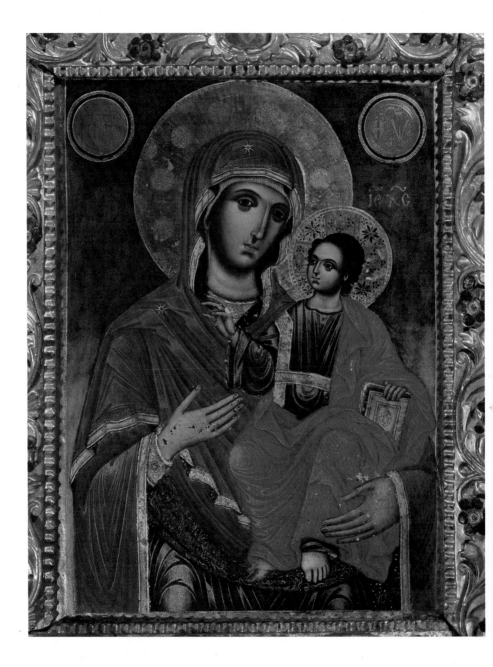

adjoin the outer stone walls and under the vaults of the entrance visitors fall under the spell of the ochre, cinnabar, green and red magnificent mosaics of ornaments, baroque scrolls, shoots and acanthus leaves concentrated on a very small surface. It is impossible to examine them in detail. They only create an impression of profusion.

There are also figural scenes. The subjects have not been randomly chosen. The scenes were painted in 1862 and feature the feats of Samson. The understatement is self-evident: the underground rumble of a coming popular uprising could be heard by all and the monastery could not turn a deaf ear to the upsurge. Its territory was a free Bulgarian land and all who came here had to get the inspiration that the whole nation needed at that point of history.

The Doupnitsa Gate with part of the monastery's facade

The monastery which was visited by many people had to provide accommodation and amenities to the pilgrims. Some Bulgarian towns had their own guest rooms offering accommodation only to their notables. The Koprivshtitsa, Chirpan, Gabrovo and Teteven rooms have been preserved to this day. They are in the north wing which is like an ethnographic exposition. The furniture, upholstery and decoration were chosen by the donors' taste; the Bulgarian towns competed with each other to outshine by their piety, prosperity and stability. The room of Koprivshtitsa whose citizens were generous donors to the monastery is the richest. The richly carved wooden ceiling of this large, almost square room is a top achievement of the baroque manner of ornamentation characteristic of Revival architecture. The supple lines make the ceiling pulsate and refract light which streams in through

An icon of the Virgin Showing the Way from the iconostasis of the Church of St Luke the Evangelist, 1799. National Museum of History, Sofia

75

The Koprivshtitsa Room (interior) - one of the guest rooms in the northeastern part of the monastery building

the many windows and radiates from the colorful couch spreads.

The monastery kitchen is on the ground floor of the same wing. The food for the pilgrims was cooked here. The kitchen is large and has an overhead opening in the shape of a huge stone chimney which goes through all the levels to take smoke from the fire to the roof and out. It is in the shape of a hollow pyramid whose walls are built by octahedrons which grow smaller. The spaces between them have been filled up by semicircular arcs. The result is an ideally balanced self-support-

ing 22-meter high construction whose lightness and strength have been proved in the course of more than a century.

The Koprivshtitsa Room - a wall painting detail

This is how the artistic reinterpretation of the building components by master builder Alexi Rilets created a true work of art, a sculpted space which still fascinates visitors .

The Rila Monastery is the material embodiment of the aesthetic ideals of the Bulgarian National Revival Period. The most prominent men of art at that time worked at the Rila Monastery. They wished to create an impressive monument of their people and their time.

The Koprivshtitsa Room - ceiling. Wood carving and decorative painting, 19th century

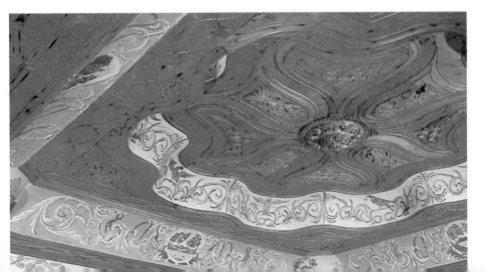

They were selfless men whose only objective had been to attain perfection for which they sacrificed their personal ambitions and even their creative uniqueness. For this reason it is difficult to decide which work belongs to which artist or group of artists although there is written evidence in the monastery archives of their involvement. This standardization, performed with an almost religious humbleness, accounts for the creation of an all-national art which had gone beyond the confines of the local art schools. In this sense the art which was created at the Rila Monastery was the first step towards the creation of Bulgarian national art.

One of the fountains in the monastery court-yard

A wood carving and wall painting composition on a ceiling, 1834

St Luke the Evangelist. A patron icon from the iconostasis of the Church of St Luke the Evangelist, 1799. National Museum of History, Sofia

THE RILA MONASTERY LIBRARY

*The Suchava Tetra-
evangelia - embossed
(front), 1529, gold and
enamel. Goldsmith
Ivan Yankov. In the
middle: Christ Cruci-
fied; the four gospel
writers are in the cor-
ners*

*Initial of a hand-written
Tetraevangelia from the
Rila Monastery Library*

That the monastery has been existing for a millennium and that the Rila monks were aware of the mission of books are the factors that produced the monastery library which can rival European counterparts. The abundant collections comprise works that have been written in the monastery, works that have been commissioned to eminent men of letters and books and manuscripts that have been donated or bought.

In the course of centuries the Rila Monastery has been the center of intensive literary activities. Outstanding educators, anonymous copyists, manuscript illuminators and book-binders spent years working there. As a result of their work today the library collection is one of the richest in the Balkans. Among the men of letters who worked at the Rila Monastery were the grammarian Spiridon, hieromonk Anastasi, Vladislav Grammaticus, Nikifor, Yossif Bradati and the great National Revival educator and champion for secular education Neophit Rilski who brought to light all old manuscripts, catalogued the library and invested a lot of effort to make it a public library which was open to the numerous pilgrims visiting the monastery.

In the 19th century Russian Slavicists showed vivid interest in the monastery's huge and extremely valuable heritage. Internationally known scholars like V. Grigorovich, A. Hilferding, F. Uspenski, P. Sirku and some others visited the monastery. Historians, literary critics and musicologists continue to study in the Rila Monastery Library and the management of the monastery provides free access and every condition for studies.

Owing to the monastic community's efforts over the centuries the library enables us to trace cultural life in Bulgarian lands in the past one thousand years.

Literary activity started probably shortly after the monastery was founded. However, extant works to prove that are not available. The earliest writings are lives of the saint of Rila. Though the extant lives are transcriptions of later dates, still they show that St John's disciples were highly educated men who were versed in the Holy Scripture and the milestones of Byzantine literature.

Between the 11th and the 14th century the Rila Monastery Library intensively acquired hand-written books. Glagolitic sheets date from the 11th century. Glagolitsa is the Old Bulgarian alphabet that Cyril and Methodius invented half a century before the Cyrillic, the other Old Bulgarian alphabet, which the Slavic nations use today but for some minor modifications. Two compiled 12th-13th century gospels on parchment have survived. The large number of 14th century hand-written books is evidence of the monastery's vivid cultural relations with the capital of the Second Bulgarian Kingdom.

A hymnography school evolved in the Rila Monastery during the 15th-18th century to compose offices to the Slav saints and promote Bulgarian poetry in the time of bondage when contacts with other Christian European countries were very limited.

The literary school which existed at the monastery during the 15th century and the centuries of Turkish domination that fol-

A page of a hand-written Tetraevangelia from the Rila Monastery Library

lowed involved several types of activities. Copyists were copying service books and mostly books containing hymns to and lives of St John of Rila. The monastery was also known for its writers and copyists of mediaeval historiography works and Bulgarian versions of church sermons (damascenes). The most interesting among them are the sermons written by Yossif Bradati who worked here ca mid-18th century. It was at that time again that the Slav-Bulgarian History, the ideological manifesto of the Bulgarian National Revival, written by monk Paisii of

A miniature from the Suchava Tetraevangelia, 1529, Rila Monastery Library

Hilendar who is said to have spent quite some time as a novice at the Rila Monastery, was copied here.

The National Revival Period transformed the Rila Monastery into a major educational and cultural center of the Bulgarian lands. The literary school evolved into an educational institution where some of the most prominent enlighteners of the nation received their education. The library opened its gates to inquisitive pilgrims and this is testified by the numerous marginal notes found in the old books. Thus very naturally it acquired the functions of a public library and paved the way to the community center libraries which became very common during the National Revival.

The Rila Monastery Library manuscript collection comprises Slavic and Greek records dating from the 11th to mid-19th century. In addition to their literary merit these records have artistic merits. Most of them have illuminations which show the Bulgarian tradition in that art. It is noteworthy that despite the large number of service books in Greek, the monastery churches and chapels never heard service in Greek although it is evident the monks had good knowledge of the language which they could speak and in which they could read and write.

The Rila Monastery collection of printed books the earliest of which date from early 16th century comprises valuable items: a Tetraevangelia from 1512 that was published in Turgovishte, books that were printed in the Venice printing house which was established in 1619, many Russian old printed books, several of the very rare editions that were printed in Vilno, of the Kievan-Pechora Laura, Moscow printed prologues. The Greek books

ЕѤѠНГ҃А СТОЕѤ

НЕПРѢ ПРОСВѢЩЕНІЕМЬ :–

ЛУ МΛО ЕѴ҃ΛΙΛΙ Х҃ВА
СН҃А БЖ҃ІА · ГАКОЖЕ Е
ПНСАНО ВЪ ПР҃ОРЦѢ · СЕ
АЗЪ ПОСНΛАѪ АГГΛА
МОЕГО ПРѢДΛНЦЕ
ТВОНМЬ, НЖЕОУГО
ТОВН ПѪТЬ ВОН ПРѢ
ТОБОѪ · ГΛАСЪ ВЪПІѪ
ЩАГО ВЪ ПОУСТЫНН · ОУ
ГОТОВАНТЕ ПѪТЬ Г҃НЬ · ПРА

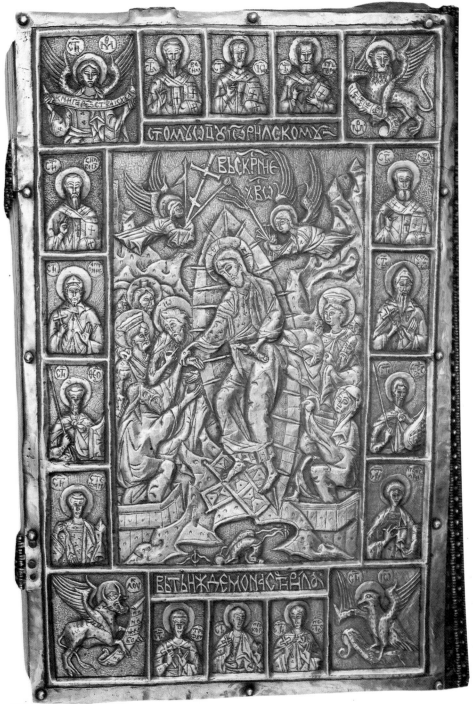

which are about 300 deal with religion, education and history.

The first Bulgarian printed books are a fine collection of their own. The Rila Monastery Library keeps Sophronius of Vratsa's Nedelnik (Weekly). Sophronius (1739-1815) was a Bulgarian bishop, writer and educator. His didactic writings in the Nedelnik illustrate the Bulgarian Revival enlightenment spirit. Neophit Rilski's two books about the worship of St John of Rila and the history of the monastery which are a must for all scholars who write about any aspect of the monastic community's prolific activity and of the writers and artists who came to work in the monastery and worked with devotion to advance this cultural center, are equally important.

The library keeps some documents from the sultans' chancellery with the signatures of sultans and highly placed officials to grant certain rights and privileges to the monastery which the Turkish authorities recognized as the major Bulgarian Christian sanctuary.

The monastery library also keeps books with the names of pilgrims who made a pilgrimage to the monastery and a donation. These books are of great historical significance. They show that the pilgrims came from Moesia, Thrace and Macedonia, ie from all lands with Bulgarian populations in the Ottoman Empire.

The Krupnitsa Tetraevangelia (embossed back), early 16th century, silver with gold. Goldsmith Matei from Sofia. The Ascension of Christ with gospel writers, apostles and Slav saints

THE MONASTERY: A MUSEUM OF BULGARIAN CULTURE AND ART

A door of the medieval Church of the Virgin of Ossenovo, 14th century. Wood carving. Rila Monastery Museum

The Rila Monastery museum collections trace its history over the centuries and reveal its role in Bulgaria's cultural history. In the course of ten centuries the Rila Monastery maintained lively relations with the countries of the Eastern Orthodox world; the metochia that were scattered in all Balkan Peninsula lands with Bulgarian population did education work; the monastery repository holds records, books, church plate, icons and gifts from pilgrims. Seeing them gives visitors today a visual idea of the past better than historians' detailed professional descriptions. The aesthetic and educational impact of those historic documents appeals to the intellect and kindles interest in Bulgarian history in the past thousand years. When a lay visitor sees them he can 'read' chapters of Bulgarian history describing the ordeals of a people who lost its freedom and gains time and again and like a phoenix risen from the ashes carried on, having learned from the ruthless lessons of history that only labor and endeavor can help survive and leave a trail in world culture and history.

The History Museum which keeps over 600 exhibits is the richest. It is on the ground floor and the basement of the newly built southeast wing. The building dates from the latter half of the 19th century and is the only structure that modern times have added to the monastery ensemble. The reason is that after the 1833 fire the monastery was almost completely rebuilt and part of the east wing

An altar cross with miniature wood carving, 17th-18th century. Rila Monastery Museum

remained unfinished. Light service buildings were put up in order to surround the court between the east and south wing and for more than 100 years, for one reason or another, they were not replaced. Today the so-called new wing stands there and houses the museum and its vaults, offices and visitors' rooms with all conveniences of a modern hotel; the architecture is in tune with the look and style of the other monastery wings but it is self-evident that it is 20th century architecture.

The Rila Monastery History Museum possesses a rich collection of extremely valuable exhibits both in the exposition halls and in the monastery vaults. The exhibits are thematically grouped and trace the evolution of the monastery and its cultural, religious and nation-consolidating role.

The exposition includes the early historical and ecclesiastical collection of the monastery, some books of the monastery library and many copies of wall paintings, original fragments from wall paintings that have been destroyed, icons, prints, vestments and church plate.

The earliest exhibits of this collection are: Glagolitic 9th-10th century sheets, the Testament of St John of Rila from the same period (in an early 19th century transcription), the saint's popular life which was written in the 12th century (in a 14th century transcription) and the Canon of St John of Rila which is a manuscript from 1789. The 14th century has bequeathed records about the feudal lord Hrelyo Dragovol who ruled the Strumitsa district. He tried to make the Rila Monastery the capital of his domain and in 1342 with the help of John Cantacuzenus he proclaimed himself an independent ruler and overthrew vassalage to the Serbian King

Stefan Dusan. Historical data are scanty and read that he 'built a magnificent monastery', to quote Vladislav Grammaticus, and a defense tower with living rooms and a chapel. The tower still rises in the center of the monastery yard. In 1335 Hrelyo Dragovol built a church which can be seen on old prints and which was destroyed in 1834 to clear site for what is today the central church. The exposition comprises the tombstone of the feudal lord with a memorial inscription which relates his dramatic death, and the wooden carved gates and throne of the Church of the Virgin of Ossenovo, one of the rare extant works of medieval church wood carving. The 14th century has left the icon of St John of Rila and the gift charter (chrysobull) of Tsar Ivan Shishman who in 1378 generously donated land, forests and estates to the monastery. The 15th century icon of St Arseni belongs to those authentic medieval documents. The characters on the tombstone, the heart-rending text, the geometric plastic carving on the doors which are some of the earliest wood carving monuments in Bulgarian lands, the faces of the saints on the two

An icon of the Virgin with the Child with reliquaries. The main church of the monastery, the small iconostasis in the northern nave

A gonfalon cross with miniature wood carving, 17th-18th century. Rila Monastery Museum

icons, the gift charter parchment, its graceful illumination and a big wax seal are visible traces of history that have survived over time which took away millions of human lives.

The Turkish domination (15th-19th century) changed life in the monastery. The earliest extant document from 1402 testifies that the government let the monastery have some privileges which did not save it from pillage ca mid-15th century. The Rila man of letters Vladislav Grammaticus whose Panegyric in the original is displayed in the Rila collection describes how the monastery was rebuilt in the latter half of the century by the three brothers and priests Joasaf, David and Theophan. A number of documents trace the monastery's relations with Mount Athos, Serbia, Wallachia and Moldova from the Middle Ages throughout the period of bondage. Relations with Russia were as active as ever. The first Rila Monastery embassy in 1558-1559 to Russia was during the reign of Ivan IV the Terrible (1533-1584). The Tsar granted a gift charter a photo copy of which can be seen in the museum. The icon of the Virgin of Vladimir dates from the same period. In the centuries that followed monk embassies many times visited Russian monasteries and rulers, as evident from the rich collection comprising over 450 Russian old printed books and from the fact that October 19 which is the feast day of St John of Rila was recorded in virtually all Russian menologies (registers of saints, with brief biographies of each, arranged according to months and days). Churches were built in Russian lands with John of Rila as the patron saint. The fine silver embossed icon of the Virgin of Kazan from 1816 is a valuable exhibit.

The Rila Monastery's centuries-long contacts with the Balkan nations are exemplified by the gifts from them: the Suchava Gospel that hieromonk Makari wrote in the Putna Monastery in 1529; the Krupnitsa Gospel that bishop Joasaf presented; the stole that Simeon, the bishop of Raska, presented in the 15th century.

The 17th-18th century, the Bulgarian National Revival, was a period in which the monastery was particularly active as a popular and cultural center. As it prospered, it opened metochia in over 50 Bulgarian towns

A detail of a gonfalon cross, 17th-18th century. Rila Monastery Museum

93

and villages. Most of them ran schools and the monks gave didactic talks in Bulgarian in the local churches. The monastery's literary work was very active owing to Yossif Bradati, Nikifor, Theophan and Paisi Rilski.

The prints, graphic impressions upon copper plates or wood, were of special significance for the popularization of the monastery and the history of its founder. There were two common types: St John of Rila with miniature scenes from his life, and the monastery itself with the main sketae and metochia along the river Rilska. Those prints were available even to the poorer pilgrims and thus popularized the Rila Monastery across the Balkan lands, serving as books for the illiterate who could learn from them the legends about the monastery and St John of Rila. Initially the monastic community commissioned the prints in Moscow or Vienna. However, as demand for such prints was growing during the 19th century, a monk Kalistrat by name was sent to Belgrade to learn the craft of print-making and in 1856 the monastery acquired a large iron press and opened its own workshop for the production of prints. The output of the latter

was large. Nevertheless the prints that it turned out were not inferior and some even could vie with art primitives.

The printing press that the monastery bought in the 1860s from Vienna is also on display in the monastery museum. The repositories keep most of the hand-made copper printing plates and prints produced with them.

The items associated with the educational activities of the ecclesiastics who constituted the core of the Bulgarian intellectuals during the early National Revival Period,

The title page of the Krupnitsa Tetraevangelia, 1577

A portrait of Neophit Rilski by Zahari Zograf, 1838. National Art Gallery, Sofia

A globe made to be a teaching aid by Neophit Rilski. Rila Monastery Museum.

reveal a very characteristic feature of the cultural process, the emergence of new Bulgarian culture in the very bosom of ecclesiastical National Revival culture. One of the exponents of that phenomenon was Neophit Rilski (1793-1881). A copy of the portrait of Neophit Rilski by Zahari Zograph, now displayed at the National Art Gallery in Sofia, is on display. The artist has portrayed this frocked revolutionary and a patriarch of Bulgarian teachers and literati with audacity, in defiance of church painting conventions and as a quintessence of the Bulgarian cultural upsurge, combining revolution and tradition in an utterly Bulgarian substratum.

The ground level halls display church plate: altar crucifixes, sanctuary lamps, censers, pyxes, archbishop croziers, miniature icons and encolpia from the 18th and 19th century.

This collection dating exclusively from the Bulgarian National Revival Period contains numerous highly artistic exhibits revealing the complex and outstandingly interesting, in terms of culture, nature of the transition from the Middle Ages to modern times. There are works of miniature wood carving, produced from the 17th to the 19th century and intended for the decoration of altar crosses, miniature icons and encolpia and for the conveyance of additional message. Some of them have been made by monks from the Rila Monastery, others have been donated. The entire collection gives an idea of the importance of this art which has not been adequately studied yet. One of the most valuable exhibits is the wooden cross carved by the resident monk Raphail over a period of 12 years, using a fine needle to carve 36 amazing compositions with more

A detail of the iconostasis wood carving in the Church of the Nativity of the Virgin

An altar cross by the monk Raphail, 1790-1802, lime wood. Rila Monastery Museum

than 200 miniature biblical figures. They say that when the monk completed his work he lost his eyesight and this envelopes the cross in romantic sadness and reinforces its impact.

The exposition includes an insignificant part of the numerous objects given as presents to the monastery and its patron saint. There are jewels, garments, weapons, everyday objects and some original abstracts from important documents. The other gifts are kept in the museum's deposit and are available only to scholars who come to the monastery to work with this incredible corpus of material.

A prominent exhibit is the huge iron safe of the monastery. The coin collection represents some of the coins that were given as generous donations by the numerous pilgrims throughout the centuries. There are ancient coins from the time of Philip of Macedon (340-315 BC); Byzantine coins from the reign of John Comnenus (1118-1143) and from the reign of Theodore III Ducas; two medallions of Emperor Constantius I, son and successor of Constantine

Christ Enthroned. 16th-17th century, wood tempera

I the Great (274-337); aspers from the reign of the Bulgarian Tsar Ivan Alexander (1331-1371); aspers from the time of his son Mihail Shishman; aspers from the reign of Ivan Shishman (1371-1393) who was the last monarch of the Second Bulgarian Kingdom. The centuries during which the Bulgarian lands were forcibly incorporated into the Ottoman Empire have endowed the monastery's coin collection with coins that were minted under 13 sultans, in addition to Venetian gold ducats, Austrian, French, Roman Catholic, British, Italian, Swiss and Russian old coins, silver groschen and gold coins that are no longer in use but are numismatically valuable.

Apart from the main exposition of the History Museum, there is a museum collection housed in some of the oldest surviving ground level premises of the north and east wings. The exposition in question shows the monastery chores. It also incorporates the monastery kitchen. Noteworthy are the large utensils which testify to the enormous number of pilgrims to whom the monastery gave food and shelter.

The old monastery canteen is a big hall with a high arched ceiling in the basement of the south wing. It displays remarkable 18th and 19th century icon painting works. Those icons are not used in the service in the Rila Monastery churches and chapels. Feast icons (featuring scenes from the feasts of saints) and the big royal doors of the iconostases are displayed in cabinets.

The monastery possesses a collection of over 100 paintings and graphic plates which feature the Rila Monastery and the Rila Mountains.

The ethnographic museum was ope-

A reliquary, 19th century, Rila Monastery Museum

ned in the 20th century to display the generous gifts to the monastery by pilgrims. It is housed in the guest rooms of the north wing. The cabinets beam with the vigor of popular art and crafts: embroidered handkerchiefs, aprons, shirts, socks and scores of belt buckles made of metal, usually silver, which were a conventional component of the Bulgarian national costume worn by women on holidays.

A tour of the four major exposition halls displaying the Rila Monastery's popular art collections will make visitors admire the inexhaustible creative ingenuity of the Bulgarians who survived and continued to create under circumstances which would have discouraged even mightier nations. They speak of the viability of Bulgarian culture.

The monastery guest rooms for one town or another that maintained relations with the monastery are part of the ethnographic museum. They are on the three levels of the north and east wing and are named after the respective town: Koprivshtitsa, Samokov, Gabrovo, etc. The exposition in each room shows the typical furnishing in a 19th century house in each of

A reliquary, 19th century, Rila Monastery Museum

An incense burner from the first half of the 19th century. Rila Monastery Museum

these towns. The room that the town of Chirpan looked after is also called Vazov's Room as the national poet, the classic of Bulgarian literature Ivan Vazov (1850-1921) liked to stay there. He wrote superb travelogues about the 'great Rila wilderness'. He passionately loved Bulgarian nature about which he wrote thus: 'I am now at home, I am in the heart of Rila.'

Another great Bulgarian, Neophit Rilski, is commemorated by two groups of premises associated with his lifework: the monastery school that he built at the Skete

A reliquary, 19th century, Rila Monastery Museum

A throne from the old church of the Rila Monastery. In the monastery museum

of St Luke, and the cells in the monastery's south wing which he occupied while he was abbot. His library is still there and shows the cultural background of the 19th century Bulgarian nation's church leaders.

Admiring the Rila Monastery as an architectural monument and as a treasure house of works of art we ought to mention with gratitude all those whose work and efforts have helped study and conserve them. Modern time has made a contribution to the history of the monastery mainly by the discovery and conservation of the architectural and artistic values, by cataloguing the manuscripts and valuable books in the library and of the documents and objects in the museum collections.

Among the historians who have made a valuable contribution to studies on and popularization of the Rila Monastery the first one who deserves mention is the great Bulgarian scholar and ardent patriot Academician Ivan Dujcev. His research work has discovered and preserved many historic documents, manuscripts and old printed books that had been saved at the Rila Monastery. Academician Krustyu Miyatev who in collaboration with Prof. Hristo Hristov and Prof. Georgi Stoikov in 1957 published the first richly illustrated study on the history, architecture, wood carvings and wall paintings at the Rila Monastery has made a major contribution too. Prof. Roumyana Radkova studied the donations made to the Rila Monastery as well as the life and work of Neophit Rilski, the eminent ecclesiastic and Bulgarian National Revival educator. Boryana Hristova studied and pub-

The Chirpan room - the ceiling

An altar cross, 19th century, Rila Monastery Museum

lished most of the library collections. A large group of museum workers worked in the monastery between 1965 and 1991 to help with the arrangement of the basic expositions of the museum collections. The inspired works of Neophit Rilski himself provide us with the most valuable information about the Revival Period monastery construction of which he was contemporary and, to an extent, a supervisor in his capacity of a member of the monastery government.

The architecture of the Rila Monastery began to be studied soon after Bulgaria's liberation from Turkish domination. The first architectural plans were made by P. Steger in 1904. Architect P. Kalchev worked later in the monastery together with a group of students in architecture. He was assisted by T. Petrov, an architect. Prof. Georgi Stoikov, an

ІС ХС
НН КК

ЕѤ Ѡ ІѠАННА СТО

ЕVАГГЕЛИЕ · ВЪ СТЖЪ И ВЕЛИКЖЪ НЕДЕЛЮ ·
И НАЧАЛО ОБѢ СЛОВО · И
СЛОВО БѢ КЪ БОУ · И БѢ
БЪ СЛОВО · СЕ БѢ ИСКО
НИ КЪ БОУ · ВЪСѢ ТѢ
БЫША · И БЕЗ НЕГО
НИ ЧТОЖЕ БЫ ЕЖЕ БЫ

ГЛА҃
УА

A page of the Souchava Tetraevangelia, 1529. Rila Monastery Library

A reliquary, late 18th century

architect, and a large group of students made a thorough plan of the monastery's accommodation buildings in 1950-1952. Again in 1950-1952 he made the plan of the Rila Monastery main church. He was assisted in that by architect C. Stoichev. The plans are the groundwork for all later conservation and restoration schemes for the monastery buildings and the central church.

Restoration was systematically carried out in the course of several decades to reinforce the monastery buildings, clean, strengthen and conserve the monastery's wall paintings and icons. Leading Bulgarian artists and restorers were involved: D. Peshev, I. Rainov, L. Krassovska, L. Mladenov, B. Ilieva, V. Zografov, Z. Kozhouharova, B. Djivdjanova, D. Kassabov and Prof. L. Prashkov, head of the Art Academy's Conservation and Restoration Department.

Their professional experience and devoted work and the efforts of scores of specialists who are so many that are impossible to enumerate, have made the monastery the cultural and tourist center that it is today with the mission to instill humanity and patriotism in contemporaries and the generations to come so that they will be able to continue the cause of the monastery in compliance with the Testament of its founder, the Rila saint.

BIBLIOGRAPHIA

1. Архив на Рилския манастир в Народната библиотека – София, папка 41, инв. ном. 4792

2. Българската литература и книжнина през XIII век. Под редакцията на Иван Божилов и Ст. Кожухаров, С., 1987, с. 49-53, 68-84.

3. Вазов, Ив. Великата Рилска обител, Сб. Народни умотворения и книжнина, 1892, кн. 7, II р.

4. Василев, А. Български светци в изобразителното изкуство. С., 1987, с. 78-100.

5. Генова, Е. Миниатюрна дърворезба XVII-XIX век, С., 1986.

6. Дуйчев, Ив. Рилският светец и неговата обител, С., 1947.

7. Дуйчев, Ив. Рилският манастир (историческо минало и паметници, С., 1960.

8. Дылевский, Н. Рыльский монастир и Россия в XVI и XVII веке, С., 1946.

9. Енчев, В. В. Из църквите около Рилския манастир, ИБАИ, IV, 1930/1931.

10. Иванов, Й. Свети Иван Рилски и неговият манастир, С., 1917.

11. Иванов, Й. Българските старини из Македония, с. 137, 171, 205, С., 1970.

12. Иванова, В., М. Коева, Пластическото богатство на възрожденската църковна дърворезба. С., 1979, с. 38-46, 156-162, 265-266.

13. Иречек, К. Рилският манастир, Пер. сп., IV, 1885, кн. 18.

14. Иречек, К. Княжество България, част II, Пътувания по България, Пл. 1899.

15. Ихчиев, Д. Турски документи за Рилския манастир, С., 1910.

16. Іеромонах Неофит Рылецъ, Описание болгарского священного монастыря Рылского, 1879, София.

17. Киселков, В. Сл. Рилският манастир, С., 1937. Поредица: Четиво по българска история, г. VI, кн. 2, 159 с. с ил.

18. Коева М., Архитектурно-композиционен анализ на църквата „Св. Богородица" в Рилския манастир – Музеи и паметници на културата, VI, 1966, кн. 1.

19. Милетич, Л. Спомен от Рилския манастир, С., 1902.

20. Миятев, Кр. Съкровищницата на Рилския манастир, ГНМ, том IV, С., 1926.

21. Прашков, Л. Хрельовата кула, С., 1974.

22. Радкова, Р. Рилският манастир през Възраждането, С., 1972.

23. Спространов, Е. Материали по История на Рилския манастир, С., 1901, Сборник за народни умотворения и книжнина, кн. XVIII, отделен отпечатък.

24. Стара българска литература. Житиеписни творби, т. IV, Съст. и редактор Кл. Иванова, С., 1986, с. 123, 543-547, 556-563.

25. Христов, Хр., Г. Стойков, Кр. Миятев. Рилският манастир, С., 1957.

26. Чавръков, Г. Български манастири, С., 1978, с. 288-303.

Margarita Koeva

RILA MONASTERY

with 85 color and 23 black-and-white photos and plans

Photographers: Vyara Kandjeva, Dimitar Angelov, Antoniy Handjiysky
Editor of the Bulgarian Text: Vyara Kandjeva
English Translation: Roumiana Delcheva

BORINA Publishing House
P.O.Box 105; 1408 Sofia, Bulgaria

ISBN 954 500 051 1

Printed by BALKANPRESS